Listening, Speaking, Viewing and Doing

BOOKS BY BILL MOORE

Organizing The Whole Language Classroom
Writing for Whole Language Learning
Reading for Whole Language Learning
Listening, Speaking, Viewing, and Doing

Words That Taste Good

Poems Please
with David Booth

Listening, Speaking, Viewing and Doing

1001 Practical Ideas
for Teaching Language Arts

Bill Moore

Pembroke Publishers Limited

© 1989 Pembroke Publishers Limited
528 Hood Road
Markham, Ontario
L3R 3K9

Canadian Cataloguing in Publication Data

Moore, Bill
    Listening, speaking, viewing, and doing

Bibliography: p.55
Includes index.
ISBN 0-921217-39-0

1. Language arts (Elementary).   I. Title.

LB1576.M6 1989   372.6′044   C89-094273-0

Editor   Frank English
Jacket & Interior Design   John Zehethofer
Typesetting   Jay Tee Graphics Ltd.

Printed and bound in Canada
9 8 7 6 5 4 3 2

Contents

Introduction

Listening and speaking are the primary language functions.

All over the world there are thousands of people who can neither read nor write, yet they cope splendidly with their environment. They know how to listen and how to talk.

Until about a hundred years ago, a very tiny percentage of the populace of most civilizations could read or write. However, they conduct their daily affairs quite well.

The criteria for the "educated" person today demand that that person be able to read and write. This is perfectly acceptable. The underlying language skills, however, are listening and speaking. We under-teach these to the peril of later learning.

The first pages deal with vocabulary. Why is this? The broader and deeper our vocabulary, the better our ability to manipulate our language; the better our ability to manipulate our language, the better our ability to think.

Thinking is in the middle of the matrix. Reading demands thinking, as does writing. Many of the so-called "reading skills" can be learned through listening. Many of the writing skills can be learned through speaking. This is because they are all thinking skills, and parts of Whole Language.

The more words we have at our disposal, the better we can express our thoughts and ideas. Much of the input here will come from literature, as well as from more factual materials. Interesting input makes for interesting output.

Playing with words is not only fun, but also essential in building up our range of word-choice. (The FUN part is important. We tend to learn best when we are relaxed; we tend to remember things learned under happy circumstances.) Much of this play with words can be done orally, and will draw from the students' background of experiences, both first-hand and vicarious.

If we can decribe something in ten possible ways, we are in a better position to write or tell an interesting story. If we can differentiate and make fine distinctions in factual matters, we are better equipped to deal with the finite world. Enlarging our vocabulary, then, is of great importance in a Whole Language approach.

Listening and speaking begin with the story or poem read or told at home. They continue in school, with storytelling, dramatizing, poetry reading and speaking. Listening and speaking can and must involve newspapers and magazines, news reports, texts and novels, as well as literature.

We listen to analyze, to be able to answer questions, to create ideas and dreams, to evaluate what is said. All this must be done through the use of interesting input. We know that the uninterested child will not listen.

We speak to inform, to entertain or to persuade. Nobody talks talking. We have to have something to talk about. A background of rich literary experiences makes this possible.

In this book we offer hundreds of ideas and activities for the furthering of the listening and speaking skills, knowing that these are an integral part of the Whole Language experience.

Listening and its attendant skill, viewing, are important for many reasons. Most of our input through life enters through the ears. Often we use both ears and eyes at once.

Most of our social interaction involves speaking, which is part of acting, storytelling and other creative endeavors.

In addition, listening parallels reading, while speaking parallels writing. Without the former skills, the latter will have slim chances of flourishing.

Viewing is a form of reading. Just as the Neanderthals read the clouds, so do we read television and movies, maps and graphics of all kinds. Television is so much a part of the lives of most children, that it is well to take a hard look at what it does, and how it does it.

Doing involves acting, reciting, storytelling and playing. It might also involve mime, singing, chanting and improvising. We express ourselves dramatically in many ways, and through this we expand our horizons and abilities.

Abilities, such as listening and speaking, viewing and doing, are hard to pin down. Some organization is needed if we are to increase our range. The children themselves must be involved here, and know not only what they are to do, but also why they are doing it, as part of their Whole Language program.

This book presents you with hundreds of activities in word-development or vocabulary-building, listening, speaking, the organization of spoken output, plus many ideas to use when watching television. In addition, there is information about drama in the classroom, and thoughts on evaluating those totally vital skills.

Words and More Words Are Basic Equipment

Vocabulary Building

In a Whole-Language classroom, the dividing lines between Listening, Speaking, Reading, Writing, Viewing and Doing are purely arbitrary. Expanding the vocabulary occurs in all phases.

Exercises for building and increasing the power of vocabulary should be a daily occurrence.

Much of the work here will be oral. We talk about words, we play with words, we manipulate our language, we increase our registers of ability with words.

Some Exercises for Building the Vocabulary

MEANING

1. Every day one or two words are chosen, from the theme on which the class is working. These are discussed: their meanings explored, the way they sound, their relatives (nouns, verbs, adjectives, adverbs, etc.). A vocabulary book is kept: individual and/or class. The more we *use* words, the more likely we are to remember them. Oral use means we can cover far more ground than with purely written assignments. Talking through word meanings is one of the most valuable exercises.
2. Expanding the above: cut up letters to spell the words we have been playing with. Students make up words from the given letters. (These could be the words we talked about, plus extras.)
3. Use each of the words in a sentence.
4. Students take the letters forming their two or three words and see how many other words they can make up from those letters.

11

5. Students learn to use idiomatic expressions (dog in the manger, under the weather, etc.)
6. Words with multiple meanings. List these and use them correctly: can, play, school, cat, dog, etc.
7. Words from names. List the words, then list explanations out of order. The students match them up.

bantam   a sort of buttoned sweater
cardigan   a small hen

8. Mix and match ways of saying things. List the words. List the alternates out of order:

turn down   encircle
go around   refuse (a job)

9. How many meanings can you give (or find) for these: air, ship, sail, plane, plain, red, can, may, trunk, wheel, etc.?
10. Words may have emotional connotations. What are the emotional connotations of these words: blue, green, yellow, red? Use them in a sentence (spoken or written).
11. Name other words for each color: e.g., blue — indigo
12. Give as many words as you can for "walk". Start with the slowest and end with the swiftest.

DERIVATIONS (LANGUAGE)

13. Words from Latin: *uno*: one — uniform, union, unite, etc.
    Give them *duo, tres, quattor* and see how many English derivatives they can find.
    Then try *annus*: year, *aqua:* water, *audio:* hear, *corpus*: body, *caput*: head, *credo:* I believe, *fortis:* strong, *magnus*: big, *pes, pedis:* foot, *primus*: first, etc. *Pedis*, for example, could give us biped, quadruped, tripod, pedal, pedestrian, etc.
14. Words from Greek: *aster*: star, *autos*: self, *bios*: life, *gramma*: thing written, *grapho*: to write, *logos*: speech, *monos*: single, *skopeo*: I see, *tele:* distance, etc. From *aster* we get asterisk, astrology, astronomy, astronaut, disaster, etc.
15. Words from Old English: *binden*: to bind, *brecan*: to break, *cwic*: alive, *sceran*: to cut, etc. From *sceran*, we get score, scrape, scrap, sharp, shear, shire, sheriff, etc.
16. Place names in North America. Study atlases. See which names came from English settlement, Scots, Irish, Welsh, Native Peoples, Greek, German, etc. For example,

Strathearne, Toronto, London, Chatham, New Hamburg, Kitsilano, Washington.

17. Place names from French: Trois-Rivières, Bras D'Or, Detroit, Des Moines, Petit Étang, etc.

18. Prefixes from Latin. While they do not work always, they usually do. If you know what they mean, you can often make an educated guess as to the meaning of the word: *cum*: with — correspond; *dis*: opposite of — disappear; etc.

19. Canadian words. Can you tell the meaning of these: bateau, cache, chowder, chipmunk, deke, Grit, mukluk, kayak, Separate School, slough, Socred? Suggest from which language they come: English, French, Indian languages, Inuit.

20. These words come from Spanish. The clue is given. Guess the word and its meaning.
    rolled tobacco leaves: c __ __ __ r
    a place where horses are kept: c __ __ __ __ l
    an outdoor seating area: p __ __ __ o
    Find more such words.

21. Here are some more words from Spanish. Have the students make up the clues for these: barbecue, cocoa, guitar, lasso, rodeo, ranch, stampede, etc.

22. Do the same with these words from Chinese: tea, ketchup, chow mein.

23. Do the same with these words from Arabic: alcohol, algebra, assassin, lemon, sherbet.

24. Do the same with these words from India: jungle, loot, pyjamas (or pajamas), shampoo.

25. Do the same with these words from North American Indian languages: moccasin, papoose, tomahawk, toboggan, skunk, etc.

26. Students use words from other languages (restaurant, pajamas, etc.) Then the history of the word is explored, using an etymological dictionary.

SYNONYMS, ANTONYMS, ACRONYMS, ETC.

Note: Any of these activities can be done orally and in writing.

27. The teacher writes the difficult "here" and "hear" on the board. Students use each correctly in a sentence, orally and in writing.

28. Find synonyms for words like: ran, said, funny, mad, etc.

29. Students make lists for: big, little, old, new, etc.
30. Have the students list these in order of size or importance.
31. Acronyms. These words are formed from the first letters of the words that name the thing described: e.g., UNO for United Nations Organization. There are no periods between the letters in an acronym. Give the students SCUBA, RADAR, NATO, OPEC, CBC, etc. Have them give others. Search the newspapers and you will find many more.
32. Homonyms: Some can be used in making up puns: write/right; sun/son; bear/bare; hoarse/horse; etc.
33. Matching synonyms. You list some words, and the students must give a synonym, starting with the letter you choose: e.g., "The word you choose must be a synonym and begin with the letter f."
    — rest on the surface of the water _ _ _ _ _ (float)
    — to do battle _ _ _ _ _ (fight)
    The students can make up more, after you have done a few. Any beginning letter can be used.
34. Do the same with opposites. This time they must start with an m.
    — Less _ _ _ _ (more)
    — Maximum _ _ _ _ _ _ _ (minimum)
    Students can make up games like this with any beginning letter.
35. Homophones: Words are pronounced alike but spelled differently (air/heir).
    Match up these homophones:
    air   awl
    sow   heir
    all   sew/so
    bare   meet
    meat   bear
36. These words all have homophones. Can you spell them? — bail, boy, braid, fair, hymn, right, raise, sun, steel, etc. You must say the homophone, spell it, and say what it means.
37. Homonyms: True homonyms are spelled alike but have different meanings. Give the two meanings for each of these: bank, bark, bear, heel, leaves, pole, tick, etc.

38. Synonyms in context. Give the students a sentence in which one word is underlined (italicized or spoken with emphasis). Have the students pick the nearest synonym from a list provided.
She bit into the *red* tomato.
— pink, yellow, hard, soft, etc.
He was a very *old* man.
— fat, ancient, blue, disgusting
39. Rank in order of power: joy, pleasure, happiness, delight, ecstasy.
40. These words can be pronounced with the accent on either the first syllable or the second. Give the meanings for both pronunciations, e.g., con*duct*: means to lead, as in an orchestra; *con*duct: means behavior.
Here are the words: present, object, rebel, etc. (The students can find others.)
41. The dictionary and thesaurus are absolutely invaluable as aids in increasing vocabulary. The dictionary is used, very often, to verify the meaning of a word. The thesaurus is used in our hunt for synonyms.
   a) Using the dictionary, give two meanings for the following words: run, office, crown, etc. Have students use each in a sentence.
   b) Using the thesaurus, find synonyms for these words: happy, big, old, famous, etc. Have the students use each in a sentence.
42. Slang is an important part of all our lives. Here are some slang words. Give their dictionary meanings and their slang meanings: trip, fuzz, neat, hunk, split, pad, crash, acid, slammer, rip off. Try to explain *why* they got their slang meanings.

COMPOUNDS

43. Students play with made-up words: astronaut, cosmonaut, cafeteria, etc. Have the students look for the root components.
44. More made-up words. Every area in life demands words, and we have made up words to use, as in sports: skateboard, stopwatch, etc. Have the students list words coming from other areas of specialization, such as television, radio, movies, etc.

45. Male and female. Add to this list: baron/baroness, buck/doe, drake/duck, emperor/empress, gander/goose, fox/vixen, husband/wife, nephew/niece, wizard/witch.
46. Parents and children. Add to this list: horse/foal, cow/calf, dog/puppy, etc.
47. Words for formal occasions. Here are some informal ways of saying things. Match them with the formal:
    — to be utterly gross   be punished for someone else's
    — to take the rap   crime
                                             act in an unacceptable manner
48. British English and American English differ. Here are some British-American and American-English names for things. Try to match them.
    British: tap, bonnet, goods wagon, guard, boot, petrol, etc.
    American: hood, gasoline, faucet, freight car, trunk, conductor, etc.
    There are many others; find some.

TRANSFORMING

49. Adding endings. Words change sound and meaning when an *e* is added to the root word. Give examples, such as mad/made, prim/prime, etc. Have the students find others.
50. Making adverbs from adjectives by adding ly, as in happy/happily. Note the spelling changes. Here are some of those new adverbs: real/really, cool/coolly. Can the students come up with a rule to explain these? Try others, such as neat, final, ready.
51. Do the same with simple, invisible, whole. Note the spelling changes. Can the students make up a rule?
52. Adjectives from nouns. You give the noun, and have the students give the related adjective. You tell them the beginning letter.
    — moon: l — lunar
    — sun: s — solar
53. Make opposites by adding a prefix, such as in grateful/ungrateful, appear/disappear, behave/misbehave, etc.

54. Plurals can be tricky. What do these have in common? — knife, wife, life, wolf, self, calf, shelf, leaf, loaf, thief, half? They are all pluralized by changing the *f* to *ves*. Thus we get *calf* changed to *calves*.

55. What do you call someone from these countries or cities? For instance, from Egypt we get the word Egyptian. Now work out the names for people from France, England, Germany, Holland, New York, Hamilton, Vancouver, Boston, Calgary, Iceland, Greece, etc.

56. Verb forms. *Lie* and *lay* demonstrate the changes that a verb goes through from one tense to another. However, the changes also result in confusions, especially with this verb. Use both forms in sentences bearing in mind that they go like this:

    Today I lie on the beach.
    Yesterday I lay on the beach.
    I have lain on the beach in the past.
    Tomorrow she will lay the table for lunch.
    She has laid the table for breakfast.
    Lie down, Spot.

COMPLETIONS

57. You give the clue and the first and last letters of the word. The students fill in the rest:
    A word that means "the opposite of": a _ _ _ _ _ m (antonym)
    A three-sided figure: t _ _ _ _ _ _ _ e (triangle)
    etc.
    This is particularly good with words that arise out of the theme.

58. What is the word? You give the students a clue and the ending. They guess the word and write it.
    "Begins with *m*. Is often seen in the Sahara Desert. Ends in *age*. (mirage)
    "Begins with *a*. Flies in outer space. Ends in *naut*. (astronaut)

59. Alphabetical sentences. Write a sentence in which each word begins with the next letter of the alphabet: e.g., At Berlin crowds danced; etc.

60. Filling in the missing letters. The students are given sentences with words from which letters have been deleted. They are to fill in the correct ones: e.g., They all fl-w away in a h-lic-o-pte-.
61. Filling in the rhyming word:
    There was a young man who said "Please,
    I have no affection for b __ __ __," (they sting), etc.

GAMES

62. Find a word that contains four *es*: teepee; four *os*: voodoo; four *gs*: giggling; four *ss*: assess or Mississippi; etc. Can you think of any other words with sets of three, four or more letters the same.
63. Play with geographical names, by looking at a map and finding peninsulas, capes, islands, estuaries, etc.
64. Find another beginning for a story, then you do not always have to start with "Once upon a time. . . ."
65. Replacing tired words. Instead of "The waves broke upon the shore", try other, more fascinating and exciting verbs, such as crashed, smashed, tumbled, boomed, etc. Replace the tired verb in this: The horses went up the hill.
66. Definition games: List the words in one column and their scrambled definitions in another. The students are to match them: miserable   peculiar
                strange   unhappy
67. Palindromes are words spelled the same backwards or forwards. You give the meaning; the students guess the word:
    even, not sloping: level
    more crimson: redder
    opposite of midnight: noon
    to peer through a crack: peep
    to blow a horn: toot
68. Let the students make up clues for the palindromes you give them. Let other students try to answer the clues. Use these: civic, Dad, Mom, pop, refer, kook, radar, etc.
69. Here are more palindromes to try: kayak, minim, rotor, Otto.

70. Names of things we eat, Give the students the clues and have them find the names of the foods. The clues are the letters of the word mixed up: e.g., *solemn* gives us *melons*.
Try these words: unpaste/peanuts, players/parsley, tressed/dessert, etc.

RELATED WORDS

71. Make lists of words to do with: agriculture, space travel, football, history, etc.
72. Stream-of-consciousness technique. The teacher writes words on the board, or says them: summer, winter.
Students jot down as many words as they can think of to describe each word; the more, the better. Quantity makes for quality, even if you have to throw out 80 percent.
73. Skim through a history text and list as many history words as possible.
74. Do the same with geography, mathematics, science, etc.
75. Special words for archeology (for example) could be: culture, fossil, dig, artifact, etc.
76. Names for containers are interesting. Here is a list of things. Name the containers you would use to transport them: e.g., beer — barrel. Now work on: legal documents, water, gasoline, coal, tea (dry), tea (wet), picnic, spare tire, airplane, six-gun, pills, sword, dead body, etc.

DESCRIBING AND EXPLAINING

77. Teacher writes nouns on the board: snow, wind, castle (only one at a time). Students write as many adjectives as possible describing each noun. These are then shared.
78. Make a three-word caption for a picture. (Brevity is not only the soul of wit, but it demands vocabulary control as well.)
79. Present a picture of a face; it shows considerable emotion. Students pick suitable words from a list to describe it. List would include such words as excited, sad, merry, miserable, glad, etc.
80. The same, only this time the students bring forth all the words. It can be done as a class lesson; it should bring out an amazing number of words.

81. Towards exactness. Have the students describe a color, smell or sound so exactly that the listener or reader gets a perfect picture or sense of the subject.

82. Here are some slightly different types of vocabulary-building activities. They call for discussion and the use of the correct vocabulary.
    a) What is a school?
    b) Make a list of things that happen in school that interest you.
    c) Describe your school building.
    d) What is good about the design?
    e) What is bad about it?
    f) What is a teacher?
    g) What is a book?

83. The Same and Not the Same.
    a) Are tables and chairs different from each other? How?
    b) Are floors and ceilings the same or different? How?
    c) Are buildings and boxes the same or different? How?
    d) Are writing and speaking the same or different? How?
    e) Are cats and dogs the same or different? How?
    f) Are trees and people the same or different? How?
    g) What is similar to television? How?
    h) How are you and I similar? How?
    j) Are we different? How?
    k) Are the people in Africa and Singapore the same as us? In which ways? How are they different from us?

84. Show the students a picture. Have them describe that picture, putting in all the details.

85. Using the imagination.
    a) You are in a strange country. All the people have wings; you do not. Describe a few moments of a typical day for you.
    b) You have landed on the moon. You fall through the crust, and discover a whole new civilization. Tell us about it.
    c) Your scientific experiment has gone wrong. You have suddenly shrunk. You are one hand tall. There is a cat in the room. Tell us about it.

86. Explaining things.
    a) Why is *ain't* considered wrong usage? Yet *aren't* and *isn't* are acceptable. What is "good" speech? Explain.

b) Make a list of your pet likes and dislikes. Try to explain them.

c) Convince me that some book, play or poem is absolutely wonderful. Make me sure that I will regret it forever if I do not read it.

CATEGORIZING

87. Teacher names categories, and the students put down as many words as they can. Categories can be: air transportation, land transportation, water-borne transportation, etc.

88. Differentiating between slang, informal language and formal language. Which words fit in which category?
   a) Nouns: fangs, choppers, teeth; bugs, creepy-crawlies, germs; micro-organisms
   b) Do the same with descriptions. He was: obese, overweight, plump, gross, etc.

89. Pick out the words that do not belong in each group.
   a) measles, mumps, factories, cold
   b) dog, cow, ship, horse
   c) dinosaur, dodo, passenger pigeon, horse

90. Picking the right one. These words are often confused with each other: principle/principal, beside/besides, less/fewer, childish/childlike, etc. Write sentences to show proper usage for each pair of confused words.

91. Parts of speech. One of the skills needed for word control is that of being able to change noun to verb, to adjective, to adverb, where applicable or possible. Make a chart and fill in the missing words.

Noun	Verb	Adjective	Adverb
punishment (students fill in the others)			
receipt			
	steal		
		happy	
			widely

21

92. Categorize under the given headings of Towns, History, Animals, Other: Medicine Hat, castles, Moose Jaw, Mesa Verde, elephants, soup, Wild West, etc.

93. Lists with a ringer. Give a list of words which fall into a specific category. One word does not fit. The students must find the word and explain why it does not belong.
   — bluebird, sparrow, gorilla, finch
   — hat, coat, banana, socks, sweater

Using these activities as a base, the students can create all kinds of games, with many of the words in daily use. Their creations could include such games as crossword puzzles and versions of Scrabble.

Listening Is the Prime Input Skill

Many studies have shown that when direct attention is paid to listening for specific purposes, and practice is conducted on these skills, improvement in ability follows.

Listening can be improved through training and practice.

Throughout the literature there is constant reaffirmation of the fact that students tend to learn and remember more through listening than in any other way.

A high percentage of all the information we get during our lives comes in through the ears.

Thus it would seem that some direct training in the listening skills is worthwhile.

Some of the Listening Skills

WITH WORDS

1. recalling the meaning of a word, in context
2. deducing the meaning of the word from the context
3. picking out the *mot juste* in any situation

COMPREHENDING GROUPS OF WORDS

4. understanding the main idea
5. understanding how details support the main idea
6. following directions
7. summarizing, organizing
8. being able to paraphrase what has been said
9. selecting the information needed from a mass of information
10. recognizing clues
11. recognizing the special language of science, poetry, etc.

EVALUATING AND JUDGING

12. seeing how what has just been heard fits with previous knowledge
13. making reasonable "educated guesses" from what is heard (inferring)

LISTENING FOR ENJOYMENT

14. interest in reading often begins with interest aroused through listening

PREPARATION FOR LISTENING

15. The teacher must listen to the students.
16. The students must be aware of the reason for listening.
17. Certain basic rules for listening must be established.
18. The emotional setting must be right. (We do not hear much when we are emotionally upset, frightened, etc.)

SOME IMPORTANT PRINCIPLES IN TEACHING LISTENING

19. All listening activities must be pleasurable experiences. Listening, above all other language skills, depends upon the readiness of the hearer.
20. Listening goes on all the time. Nevertheless, specific listening activities must be planned for every day. These can be used with the whole class, with small groups, or with individuals.
21. The teacher is not the sole fount of knowledge in the room. Opportunities must be made for the students to do much of the talking. Students learn more from each other than from the teacher.
22. Whenever we ask students to listen, they should be listening *for* something.

Who Is a Good Listener?

A good listener is one who:
1. knows how to listen, and actually concentrates on listening.
2. is selective.
3. can grasp and talk about:
   main idea
   supporting details

cause and effect
fact and opinion
sequence
figurative language.
4. is a critical listener; is not swayed by catchphrases and obvious propaganda.
5. is courteous towards the speaker, and to other listeners.
6. is able to zero in on the speaker and eliminate extraneous noise and interruption.
7. remembers what has been said.
8. asks himself or herself questions while listening, constantly checking his or her knowledge with the ideas presented.
9. anticipates what is coming next.
10. evaluates while listening.
11. recapitulates from time to time.

Here Are Some Listening Activities

They could be done in groups, with the whole class, or individually.

ANALYSIS

1. listening to a paragraph: students answering questions on it (main idea, cause and effect, sequence, detail, etc.)
2. answering true-or-false questions
3. answering multiple-choice questions
4. looking for clue phrases in a speech (in summary, thus we see that, to recap let me say, sometimes, after this, while this was happening, etc.)
5. guessing the story line from hearing the title
6. listening to analyze mathematics problems (What are we given? What do we have to do? etc.)
7. analyzing reports (of a game, a trip, etc.)
8. examining evidence to decide one way or another (Was Tom right to do this? Was the battle at . . . a victory for this or that side?
9. listening to a news broadcast and analyzing its bias, or its lack of bias
10. listening to solve riddles
11. listening for sequence
12. listening to pick holes in commercials and political promises

13. getting the meaning of the words from the context (Many animals hunt by day, but the tiger is a nocturnal hunter. What does "nocturnal" mean?)
14. listening for the *mot juste* in a poem or story
15. listening to pick out the "purr" and "snarl" words used in propaganda
16. listening to pick out rhyming words

REPORTING

17. making notes as the speaker continues speaking
18. summarizing
19. paraphrasing
20. listening to pass information on to others (must be correct in details)
21. listening to make notes in point form
22. listening to a story so that we can make up a sequel

INFORMATION AND PLEASURE

23. listening for pleasure (to a poem, a story, a piece of music)
24. following directions — from the simplest to the most complicated
25. listening for facts and opinions
26. listening for character analysis in a story

READING

27. listening to a story on tape, while reading along from a script
28. listening to a whole story on tape, and then trying to read it by oneself

The Listening-Reading Connection

Many of the above exercises employ many of the skills we traditionally think of as "reading comprehension skills".

In reading, the information comes in through the eyes, while in listening it comes in through the ears. Both are input, and their similarities can be exploited to the enormous advantage of the student.

Listening is usually a more relaxed activity than reading. The demands are slightly less rigorous, and most students tend to be relaxed. Many students who are poor at reading are very good at listening. This gives them a chance to shine, which at the same time reinforces their feeling that they can do certain things very well. This is why listening should be employed in teaching so many of the reading skills.

Ways in Which Listening and Reading Are Very Much Alike

1. Both are input activities.
2. Both involve thinking, and applying what is already known to the unknown.
3. Both involve the interpreting of words and groups of words.
4. Both require discrimination.
5. Both demand some degree of concentration.
6. Both can have a raison d'être.
7. We read for information, for enjoyment or to be persuaded. We listen for those same reasons.
8. Both ask for the ability to anticipate.
9. Both demand that we assess what is being presented, from time to time.
10. Both demand that we ask ourselves who the speaker is and why the speaker is making such statements. (A healthy dose of cynicism is needed in this age of constant t.v. and radio overkill.)

Discuss these ideas with your students.

Get them to make up lists of *dos* and *dont's* for listening.

Nearly everyone has a far larger listening than reading vocabulary. The transfer of words from the listening to the reading vocabulary can be made if we have plenty of organized listening activities.

Speaking Demands Structure

Classroom talk is essential. The silent classroom may not be the most efficient. Students must be given opportunities for speaking. These must be structured, or the exercise degenerates into futility.

It is generally conceded that the better a person's ability to manipulate the language, the better that person's ability will be to think.

The more opportunities we give students to manipulate language, the better we are preparing them for the thinking skills of reading and writing.

Advantages of a Planned Program

1. The language skills develop faster.
2. Most people have a higher level of ability in speaking than in writing.
3. Most people have a larger speaking vocabulary than writing vocabulary.
4. The sheer amount of talking we can do is greater, within a restricted time limit.
5. We do not seem to be as critical of speaking errors as we are of writing errors.
6. When people speak, there is often immediate feedback from the listeners.
7. Talking is a social and socializing activity.
8. Talking is a perfect lead-in to writing. Many of the same skills of organization are used.

9. Language is made up of sounds, not letters. Writing is a dependent skill.
10. Native speakers control most of the elements of language before they come to school.

Structured Storytelling

A story, told by the teacher, is the best way to start the language flowing with students.

In a story, there is no problem. No personal information is brought forth. There is structure, which is invaluable, and absolutely essential, if we are to write consecutive material later on.

Here is a suggested technique:

1. Teacher tells the story. (Pick up a simple legend or folktale, intended for oral presentation.)
2. Teacher and students recap the story, noting main points in word or picture form. These mnemonics are the beginning of planning for a story or an essay.
3. Teacher retells the story.
4. Students work in pairs, each telling the story to the other.
5. Repeat this activity.
6. Move from storytelling to interviewing. One of each pair is the interviewer, the other is a main character from the story. The interview takes place one day after the story ends.
7. Interview both a major and minor character from the story. This might include the protagonist and the antagonist. Here we get point of view, a very important literary skill.
8. The next step could be dramatization.
9. If the need is felt, the script could be written down for use as a playscript.
10. With experience, many of these steps could be telescoped.

While the pairs are working, the teacher moves among them, picking up excellent use of vocabulary, phraseology, etc. This is shared with the whole class later. Depending on the level of sophistication within the class, the amount of time spent will vary. A good rule of thumb is: keep the sessions brief. Five minutes is a good maximum.

Talk and More Talk: Structured Activities

Here are some activities to promote talk. They could be used for discussion by pairs, by small groups or with the whole class.

SCHOOLS

1. What is a school?
2. What is supposed to happen in a school?
3. Make a list of things that happen in school which interest you.
4. Make a list of those you dislike and tell why.
5. Describe your school building.
6. Describe the surrounding area.
7. What is good about the physical design of the school?
8. What is bad about it?
9. What is a teacher?
10. Describe the best teacher you have ever known. (no names!)
11. What is a book?

SAME/DIFFERENT

12. Are all books the same?
13. Are tables and chairs different? How?
14. In which ways are floors and ceilings the same/different?
15. In which ways are buildings and boxes the same/different?
16. In which ways are writing and speaking the same/different?
17. In which ways are dogs and cats the same/different?
18. In which ways are trees and people the same/different?
19. What does television resemble? In which ways?
20. What does a pencil resemble? How?
21. How are you and I alike/different?
22. In which ways are the people in Africa the same as us?
23. In which ways are we different from the people in Austria?

DESCRIPTION

Use a picture . . . magazine cover, etc. Let the students look at it carefully, then ask them to discuss:

24. What is happening?
25. Who is doing what to whom?
26. Where are they doing it?
27. How are they doing it?
28. Why are they doing it?

29. What is the picture supposed to make you feel?
30. Now, describe the picture to someone who has not seen it. He or she should be able to draw a rough copy, including the major points.
31. Describe an object you are holding in your hand. The listener must draw a sketch of the object. The better your description, the more accurate the sketch will be.
32. Use your imagination: You are in a country where all the people are blind. You are not. Describe a typical morning.
33. You land on a planet, and fall through the crust. There is something amazing underneath. Tell us about it.
34. You have suddenly shrunk to one centimetre high. A dog comes in.

EXPLAINING

35. Why is *ain't* considered wrong?
36. What is grammar?
37. List your pet hates. Explain them.
38. You get a book from the library. What made you choose it?
39. Should you read every book that you get through to the end? Why?

PERSUADING

40. Convince me that this book, play, t.v. show, poem, story is the best ever, and that I have to read it, or my life will be incomplete.
41. You are in a store with your best friend. After you leave the store, the friend shows you something he/she has stolen. What do you do?
42. One of your friends offers you a piece of a stolen chocolate bar. What are your reactions?
43. You find a ten-dollar bill on school property. Reaction?
44. You find a ten-dollar bill downtown. Reaction?
45. Your friend admits stealing something. An unpopular classmate has been accused of the crime. What do you do?
46. You have been told to be home by a certain hour. You think that is unfair. (One student be the parent; the other be the child. Argue.)
47. Your parents are going to X for the holidays. You do not want to go. Argue your case.
48. You are short-changed in a store. The clerk is an old lady. Reaction? What do you say?

49. The same situation, only the clerk is a young, good-looking member of the opposite sex. How do you react?
50. The clerk is a friend of your family. Your reaction?
51. The clerk is someone your family does not like. Your reaction?

MAKING RULES

52. Make a list of the ways in which you had to conform when you were little. In pairs, decide which rules could now be amended.
53. Some conformity is essential in school. Discuss this. (One student takes a pro stand, the other takes a stand against the argument. Try switching sides as well.)
54. List three basic rules for your classroom to operate efficiently.
55. Discuss this statement: Sometimes there is not time for democracy.
56. "What if" situations:
    a) What if all the plastic in the world disintegrated?
    b) What if the sun stopped shining?
    c) What if all the water froze?
    d) What if the mean temperature in your town suddenly rose ten degrees?
    e) What if you could keep only five books? Choose. Tell why.
    f) What if you found yourself in a place where nobody understood your language? What would you do? How could you help someone from another land who was in that situation?

Speaking From Outlines

"Speaking" used to be called Oral Composition, which means speaking in some sort of structured, organized fashion.

Here are some outlines for speeches on various topics. This outlining is a form of planning, and is a wonderful lead-in to planning for written compositions.

Begin with a speech on a topic well-known to everyone: myself.

Outline

We always begin with the *address*. This could be: "Mrs. Brown and Classmates"; or "Madam President, Ladies and Gentlemen"; or whatever suits the occasion. The address is important, just as the opening salutation in a letter is important. Formality, like this, helps to set the pattern. Then carry on by introducing the topic: "I am going to talk to you awhile about 'Myself'."

1. name
2. where born
3. when born
4. something about that place, if significant
5. where now
6. what doing now
7. school
8. subjects (with comments as needed)
9. hobbies, outside connections, clubs, etc.
10. family
11. particular interests now
12. ambitions for the future

Note: Outlines are wonderful. If you forget any step, you can put it in later. You can leave out any step that might be boring or embarrassing.

A FAMOUS PERSON

Here we can follow a similar outline:
Address
1. name of person
2. where and when born
3. something about place, if significant
4. where now
5. what doing now/why famous
6. how became famous; steps along the way
7. family etc., if significant
8. most important contribution to the world
9. plans for future (if applicable)

   This kind of outline could be used for a talk about any person in history, such as Christopher Columbus, Ferdinand Magellan, Francis Drake, John A. Macdonald, Wilfrid Laurier, George

Washington, Theodore Roosevelt, Terry Fox, etc. It could be used also for a talk about a fictional character, such as Robin Hood, King Kong, Br'er Rabbit, Charlotte (of the Web), etc.

NAMES IN THE NEWS

Address
1. name
2. where from? when?
3. why in the news?
4. present position
5. why doing/what doing; world opinion/my opinion
6. important background information
7. possible results of this action

Note: Once more, some sections may be eliminated if not applicable.

COUNTRY IN THE NEWS

Address
1. name of country
2. where (use map if need)
3. any significant points in history of country
4. why in news now
5. why this happened . . . world opinion/my opinion
6. possible outcomes

This is a good way to share information in a Current Events program.

BOOK REPORTS

Address
1. title
2. author, publisher, date
3. main plot of book
4. characters and setting
5. most interesting part (to me)
6. read a little section
7. why I like this
8. personal comments

Many of these outlines could be used in a personal teacher-student interview. It might be wise to have the student do one of these with you, before asking the student to speak before the whole class. Once a routine is established, most students will find that the outline gives them confidence.

There is a vast difference between this and the usual "oral composition", where the student *reads* a prepared script, sometimes actually written for him by some helpful or hopeful adult.

After doing several of these, ask the students to help you prepare a class outline for a talk on things such as:
My Favorite T.V. Show; Here Is a Film You Must Not Miss; The Discovery of Insulin; How Humans First Learned to Fly; etc; etc.

Introducing a Speaker

Once students are using outlines, such as those suggested above, it is time to have speakers introduced. Here is an outline that will fit any speaker:

Address (This will include the speaker's name first, as a courtesy: "Dr. Livingstone, Madam President, Girls and boys," or "Miss Nightingale, Mr. Chairman, Ladies and Gentlemen," etc. This formality is helpful. We are always more comfortable when we work within a structure. It also happens to be the correct thing to do!)
1. name of speaker
2. where from (place or idea, famous Space Centre, etc.)
3. topic speaker will talk on
4. qualifications of speaker
5. "We will enjoy, find interesting," etc.
6. speaker's name again
   A typical introduction might sound like this: "Captain Smith, Miss Green, fellow students; this morning it is my happy duty to introduce to you Captain William Smith of the Salvation Army. He is going to tell us about his experiences running a leper colony in West Africa. He is amply qualified to speak on this topic, as he directed such a hospital and colony in Mozambique for 20 years, and was assistant director of a similar place in East Africa for ten years before that. I know we will find what he has to say most interesting and informative. Here is our speaker: Captain William Smith."
   Again, if the introducer leaves a step out, it can be put in later. If some steps are inappropriate, they can be left out.

Such an outline will produce a speech that will take less than one minute. That is desirable. The introducer's job is simply to bridge the gap between the known audience and the unknown speaker. The shorter, the better.

Thanking a Speaker

Address. (Again, use the speaker's name: "Captain Smith, Madam President, Ladies and Gentlemen...")
1. On behalf of. . . .
2. Thank.
3. Make mention of something specific in the talk, that you especially liked.
4. Thank again.

(Should we say, "Please come and speak to us again?" Only if we truly mean it. Never lie.)

ACTIVITIES

Have the students make outlines for: presenting a soccer prize; thanking for a volleyball cup; presenting an award for the best. . .; thanking, on behalf of the school, for . . . given by the Kiwanis Club; etc.

Planning a Longer Speech

Get the *middle* in shape *first!*
  Ask yourself these questions:
1. Who is the audience to be? (We will plan differently for a Grade one group and a group of parents.)
2. What do I want to do? (Inform? Persuade? Amuse?)
3. What are my main points?
4. What supporting details do I need?
  Every talk must have a beginning, a middle and an end.

The Middle of the Speech

There are three main ways to organize the middle of the speech:
1. Chronologically
2. Logically
3. Building to a climax

The best way to organize is this:
1. Collect all the material and information you need. Jot it down as it comes. This is often called the "heap of ideas".
2. Look through your heap of ideas, and select those you are going to use.
3. Organize these into some pattern.

The Middle should be organized first. Decide on your opening and closing afterwards.

The Opening of the Speech

This must grab the attention of the audience. We must spend some time thinking up an interesting opening. Here are some ways:
1. A startling statement (If people had had refrigerators, Columbus might never have sailed the ocean blue!)
2. A question (Why did Columbus sail the ocean blue?)
3. A quotation (In 1492 Columbus sailed the Ocean Blue.)
4. A personal reference (I have always been fascinated by Columbus.)
5. State your purpose. (Before you leave today, you will know more about Columbus than you did before.)
6. An anecdote
7. A picture
8. Some other concrete materials

Often, we combine two or more of the above.

Have the class practice openings on these topics. They do *not* do the whole speech — just the openings. Try to use as many as possible of the eight types above.

1. Francis Drake
2. Wayne Gretzky
3. The Panama Canal
4. Our town
5. My favorite animal
6. My trip to Disneyworld/Wonderland
7. My first ride in a jet plane
8. This book changed my life
9. My pet skunk
10. Crossing guards
11. The world's largest swimming pool
12. The Olympic Games
13. How to catch fish
14. My hobby
15. How the hockey team won last night
16. Learn to use your camera
17. Municipal elections
18. The United Empire Loyalists
19. The school library
20. My uncle — the ballet dancer

Closings

The end of a speech is almost as important as the opening. It should be carefully prepared.

Here are some suggestions:
1. A general summary of what you have said
2. A reference to your main points ("And so we see that because of this . . . that happened"; "because of this . . . that happened.")
3. Repeat the introduction.
4. Refer to the introduction.
5. Look into the future.
6. Make an appeal for the listeners to *do* something.
7. Use a quotation different from the opening one.

Some of these will, obviously, apply more to one speech than another.

Practice closings for these topics. Do *not* do the whole speech:
1. All the topics suggested above
2. Each student writes the title of a speech. These are put into a hat, and each draws a topic, for which he or she must design a closing.

The Impromptu Speech

There is value in giving impromptu talks. This is a wonderful way to get used to using words, and in organizing on the spot. Impromptu talks will be quite brief.

Here is a possible way to organize an impromptu talk:
1. Grab the listeners' attention right away. (some of the opening ideas above, plus any others you can think of)
2. Make sure you make the listeners feel that there is something in it for them.
3. Get to your main point right away.
4. Give some examples to support your main point.
5. Wrap it up smartly. (Use some of the ending ideas above, plus new ones.)

Here are some topics for Impromptu talks:
1. All and any of the above
2. What this school needs
3. Comic books are not funny.
4. The driving age should be lowered.
5. It happened to me last night.
6. What is on next week at the local moviehouse.
7. My cat, dog, canary, hamster, etc.
8. Don't ever get a hamster.
9. Why you should buy my bike
10. How to make pocket money, etc.

Viewing and Doing — Television and Drama

Listening and *reading* are *input skills*. Viewing is an input skill, analogous to listening and reading. Many of the skills involved in listening and reading are used in *viewing*.

Speaking and *writing* are *output skills*. Doing is an output skill, analogous to speaking and writing. Many of the skills used in speaking and writing are used in *doing*.

Most students spend a great deal of time viewing television. It can be a waste; properly handled, it can be a useful educational tool.

Television Viewing Activities

Here are some ideas for making use of *viewing* television. Most of these could apply to any other type of viewing. In many cases *doing* is included, as are Listening, Speaking, Reading and Writing.

T.V. CHARACTERISTICS

1. Discuss with the class the differences between viewing t.v. and reading a book.
2. In a book, we can go back to savor a passage, or reread something to make it clearer. Can we do the same with t.v.?
3. Get someone from a local t.v. station to talk to the class about t.v. production: the role of the producer, director, script person, camera people, floor manager, etc.
4. Visit a t.v. station (many communities have local cable t.v. stations).
5. Keep a continuing list of t.v. terms.

6. List programs that inform you. How can you find out if the information they give is true?
7. List the science, geography, history shows that have taught you something.

LOG BOOK AND SCHEDULES

8. Each student is to keep a log for one week, listing everything viewed. Discuss.
9. Keep an ongoing Television Bulletin Board. On it, list programs you think others will want to watch: educational programs of value coming up, reviews of programs seen, books that have been made into t.v. shows now available, books and magazines related to some big event to be seen on t.v., science programs of special and timely interest, etc.
10. Some shows are on too late at night for young people to watch. Write your local t.v. station and suggest changes to their schedules. (Most t.v. people are willing to reply and do so courteously.)

VIOLENCE

11. Discuss violence on t.v. shows. Why do the characters all seem to recover so quickly after fights? Why does no one ever look particularly bad after a fight?
12. Using a video cassette of a show in which there is much violence. Before viewing, talk about violence, the different types, etc. Prepare a viewing guide, watch the tape and then discuss.
    Suggested viewing guide:
    Name of program:
    How many killings:
    How many shootings:
    How many beatings:
    How many fires:
    How many car crashes:

13. Violence is usually thought of as physical. It can also be verbal (abuse). Keep a log for a week, listing violence in these categories and the name of the show:
Physical Violence   *Verbal Abuse*   *Show*

Then discuss class reactions.
14. Talk to a local police officer about his or her work. How does it differ from the t.v. version?
15. "The way people beat up on each other on t.v. suggests to most young people that hitting, knifing and shooting others is the normal way of settling differences." Discuss.
16. List incidents of verbal abuse in the programs you see in one evening.

DISCUSSION

17. Watch an interview show. Use the format to run an interview show in your classroom.
18. Hold panel discussions about t.v. talk shows (and other shows) that you have seen or will be seeing.

COMMERCIALS

19. Discuss commercials, under the topics of: what, why, how, when, etc.
20. What do you like or hate about some commercials? How are some commercials funny? Which commercials do you find good? What makes them good or bad?
21. We see commercials everywhere. List commercials that have made you think a product was much better than it really was. Write a letter to the t.v. station, expressing your feelings.
22. List five "honest" commercials.
23. Turn off the sound while watching a commercial. Could you understand the message? Try to write the script for this, or any other, commercial.

VALUES AND INFLUENCES

24. List programs that insult your intelligence.
25. List programs that make you think.
26. Discuss how t.v. influences our feelings about other people.
27. Discuss how t.v. can influence the way we feel about ourselves.

28. Television gives us many pictures of family life. These are often quite different from ours. Pick one show, view it and discuss how the family is like ours and how it is different.
29. Why are these families unlike ours?
30. Pretend that you are from Mars. All you know about earth is what you have seen on t.v. sitcoms. You have been asked to talk about earthlings and their lives. From what you have learned from watching t.v., talk about: a typical family, the houses people live in, the weather on earth, what fathers do, what mothers do, what children have in the way of clothes, toys, privileges, etc., how many people are handicapped, how many white, yellow, brown and black people are there, which kinds of foods people eat, where they eat, which kinds of accents they have, what they do that we cannot do, etc. This will lead into discussions of truth and stereotyping.
31. Stereotypes abound on t.v. Use this list as a starter, and jot down stereotypes that you notice as you watch for a week.

Stereotype	Show	Comments
childish woman		
stupid father		
ugly, bad guy		
domineering parent		
overly smart child		
revolting child		
pathetic old person		
goody-goody child		
untrustworthy adult		

32. On the other hand, can you find any of these in sitcoms or dramas on t.v.? List them and the show that presents them. Life roles: a working mother, a mother who is brilliant, a handicapped person who leads a full life, a teenager who is not wild about rock groups, a studious young person, an active grandmother or grandfather holding down a good job, a man doing housework, etc.
33. Why are there so many stereotypes on t.v.?
34. Who do you admire most in the field of sports? Why?

EVALUATING AND CATEGORIZING

35. Just as we read different materials in different ways, so we view differing t.v. shows differently. Discuss types of t.v. programs, such as sitcoms, news, news specials, documentaries, sports, game shows, drama, etc.
36. Make lists of favorite programs. Have each student keep a notebook in which these are listed. From time to time, have each student give a review of one program seen the night before.
37. Discuss truth and fiction in t.v., and where each overlaps the other.
38. Certain types of programs do not appeal to many students. Some of these are quite valuable documentaries. Have the class view one of these and note its good and bad points. Discuss.
39. Write letters to t.v. stations about your likes and dislikes in their programming.
40. Discuss fantasy programs, like "Super-anyone". Why do we like them? Are these people real? Are they believable? Why?
41. Read a book, then watch a film based on it. Which do you prefer? Why?
42. Make a list of characters from t.v. shows. These might be real actors or cartoon characters. Tell your favorite and why.
43. List your favorite sports programs. Why do you like these? What do you like best about these programs? What do you wish could be changed?
44. List five ways in which t.v. has been good for you.

STORYTELLING AND SCRIPTING

45. Use t.v. to teach sequence, cause and effect, story line, foreshadowing, etc.
46. Compare a taped news story on t.v. with the same story in the newspaper. What does each type lack? In which ways is each one superior?
47. Write a different ending for a sitcom you have just seen.
48. Write a 50-word synopsis of a show you have seen.
49. Write a 50-word synopsis for a show you would make from a story or book you have read.
50. Write a 50-word synopsis for a documentary on some subject dear to you: pollution, modern art, baseball, fashion design, etc.

51. Learn how a t.v. script looks: audio on one side, video on the other. Take a simple play script from a book and convert it into a t.v. script.
52. In groups, or individually, make up a story about a superhero. You can use all the special effects you want in your t.v. script.
53. Take a large piece of paper. Fold it into four squares. Use these four squares to show some specific action of your superhero. The dialogue could be printed beneath.
54. Pretend you are writing a new t.v. show. You want the viewers to hate one character. What will you do to make that character loathed? Consider looks, clothes, speech, actions, etc.
55. Do the same with a character that you want us all to love.

GAMES

56. Play "Who am I?" Each person is a character from t.v. Each talks about himself or herself, in character, but never gives the character's name. Each could act out the character. Others then try to guess which character is being presented.
57. Do the same thing in written form. Each student writes a "Who am I?" piece, and does a drawing of the character. The drawings and writings are put up around the room. Students are to match the writing and the drawing.

Note: Many of these activities could be done with film, newspapers, magazines, etc.

Dramatizing

Dramatizing a story is a valuable activity and there are several ways of doing this:
1. Take a story and use the dialogue, with a narrator giving linking bits of text.
2. Take a story; divide it into scenes; and ad lib each scene. Every time it is done, the words will be slightly different.
3. Dramatize a poem.
4. As an introduction to a poem, dramatize the situation, then read.
5. Dramatize as a follow-up to the poem (sequel, different ending, outgrowth, etc.).

6. Take characters from poems or prose. Dramatize their stories through interviews, scenes, etc.
7. Monologues: be one character from a play, poem or story, and tell your tale.
8. Perform a poem on videotape. Add music to make it more interesting.
9. Do "Jack and the Beanstalk", "Cinderella", "Snow White", etc., as a video. Scenery, costumes and sound effects will add extra dimensions.
10. Mime along with a narrator's reading of a story or poem.
11. Use puppets to present the action.
12. Tell a story through tableaux (a series of frozen pictures, with a narrator).
13. Choral reading with solos, small groups and whole choruses.
14. Write a script for a stage version of a story or poem.
15. Write a script for a t.v. video of the piece.
16. Present the piece to an audience (younger children, parents, other classes, etc.).

Some Suggestions for Doing a Scripted Play

When we dramatize, we take an idea and make a play out of it, using many of our own words. Every time we do the dramatization it is slightly different.

Sometimes we like to work with a scripted play. In this case, the words are the same every time we do it.

Often, classes rush into a scripted play, and try to act it out before they are ready. Here is a suggested plan to follow, when you are using a script.

1. Talk with the class about the play, setting the scene, the time, the sort of play it is.
2. Have them read through the play silently.
3. Have them answer questions on the play. Make them simple, as the questions are really to make sure that they have grasped the main elements of the plot. Often a quiz sheet is useful at this point.

4. Talk about the answers to the quiz. This sets the sequence of the play, the characters, etc. Discuss the characters. Sometimes it helps to ask who would fit certain characters, if we could use any actors from movies or t.v.
5. The students now must reread the play silently. This is the hardest step, as they all think they do not need to. Some sort of quiz on this helps them to reread. Ask questions which are slightly different from the first round. Open-ended questions are useful.
6. Discuss the play. Now get them thinking about setting, characters, how they feel, how they should be dressed, etc. Visualizing is important, because a play is a three-dimensional, living thing.
7. Now we read the play aloud, sitting in our seats. How do we make sure that everyone is involved: 30 students, and a play with five characters? Read only a page or so at a time. Wherever it seems natural to cut, stop; and have different students read different characters. (This time, Charlie, you be Captain Hook; Mary, you be the Princess; etc.) Each scene is read, with different students taking parts, several times. You could do it cumulatively: do Scene One several times; then do Scene Two several times; then do Scenes One and Two together; etc. This might sound tedious. Actually, it is not, and it allows students to become so familiar with the script that, when they try standing up and doing a scene, with movement, etc., they are at ease.
8. Having read all the scenes aloud many times, we are now ready to begin acting. Divide the scenes as before: from the beginning to the middle of page 2 (often this can be a natural breaking spot, where a new character enters, or someone leaves). When that is done, repeat the scene with two different students taking the parts. Scene One, repeats; then Scene Two, repeats; then Scenes One and Two; repeats; and so on.

In this way, everyone gets a chance to perform.

Once your students are sophisticated in this mode, you can adapt. For instance, Steps 7 and on could be done in small groups, etc. Sometimes you can telescope steps; but never go into Step 7 before some preliminary work.

If you follow a scheme like this, every student can be involved, and the final acting will be enjoyable and good.

Should we ever proceed to presenting the play? Certainly, if it is good for the students' development. Even if you present the play to the public (older or younger children, parents, etc.) always switch characters from scene to scene, so that everyone gets a chance.

Evaluation

Evaluating Speaking and Listening

The evaluation of students' speaking and listening abilities can be made less vague if we use certain forms, such as these:

Outline for Marking Student Speaking and Listening

a) The student gains and maintains the attention of others.
b) The student uses adults and others as sources.
c) The student can express ideas and emotions clearly.
d) The student can lead where necessary, and follow where necessary.
e) The student can converse naturally with peers and teachers.
f) The student can use spoken language to
   control a situation;
   to share information;
   to use the imagination.

Remember always: *Evaluation deals with growth.*
Evaluation must be ongoing.

Log-Type Appraisals

LOG-TYPE APPRAISAL FORMS (USED BY TEACHER)

0900: chats with friends before bell . . . laughs often . . . helped Mary find her book . . . etc.
0930 had trouble understanding arithmetic problem . . . was not willing to talk it through with me yet. . .
1315 had fight in schoolyard . . . crying when came in . . . "I'm going to murder that Ken. . ." etc., etc.
This is a running record, and obviously we cannot keep one for every student for every day.

Here we have a form that the teacher fills in:

Log showing student talking and listening with other students

Name   Date   Subject Area Observed

a) ignores
b) aware, but not involved
c) initiates
d) co-operates
e) directs well
f) follows directions

LOG SHOWING INTERACTION WITH TEACHERS

Name   Date   Subject Area Observed

a) reluctant to speak or listen
b) easy/confident
c) responds well
d) responds poorly — monosyllabic
e) can maintain talk
f) contributes well as group member
g) tends to dominate groups using bully tactics

Checklists and Other Evaluation Forms

OBSERVING STUDENT'S LISTENING AND SPEAKING

Name   Date   Subject Area Observed   Good   Fair   Poor

a) attention span
b) participation
c) follows directions
d) gives directions
e) listens to other students
f) joins in small-group activities
g) knows how to paraphrase information

OBSERVING RICHNESS OF STUDENT'S LANGUAGE

| Name | Date | When Observed | Comments |

a) natural, easy, colorful language
b) good awareness of listeners
c) obviously understands what is said by others
d) shows interest
e) can suit language to the occasion
f) can give ideas briefly
g) is organized in output

LISTENING AND SPEAKING

| Name | Date | When/Where | Comments |

a) grasps main idea
b) can use details to support argument
c) can understand and apply sequence
d) can follow directions
e) catches the emotional meaning

STUDENT SELF-CHECKLIST

a) Do I listen more than I talk?
b) Do I listen all the time/some of the time/none of the time?
c) What distracts me?
d) Am I organized in my talk?

OBSERVING STUDENT IN GROUP SITUATION

(Could be used by teacher or other student)

| Name of Observer | Student Observed | Date |

a) student paid attention while others spoke
b) took part in discussion
c) distractive behavior of student
d) asked questions
e) could disagree without anger
f) put ideas over well
g) vocabulary

LISTENING FOR SPECIFIC REASONS TO A LONG TALK OR READING

a) Can student write or speak a précis or paraphrase?
b) Can student ask good questions afterwards?
c) Can student follow any directions?
d) Can student report back what was heard?
e) Can student take notes while listening?
f) Can student allow for bias, point of view, etc.?

SPEAKING BRIEFLY

a) Can the student make announcements?
b) Can student introduce and thank speaker?
c) Can student give instructions well?
d) Can student tell the story of a book?

SPEAKING AT GREATER LENGTH

a) Can the student build an outline?
b) Is the student's opening and closing good?
c) Can the student reach his or her audience?

READING ALOUD

a) Does the student understand the meanings of the words?
b) Does the student understand the emotional tone of the words?
c) Does the student use the appropriate speed?
d) Does the student read with appropriate use of phrasing, rhythm, tone, inflection?
e) Does the student use correct inflections, articulation, enunciation, pronounciation?
f) Is the reader loud enough? Quiet enough?
g) Is there variety in the reading?

STORYTELLING

a) Was the opening effective?
b) Did the story interest the listeners?
c) Was the voice used to create different characters?
d) Were the climaxes reached and obvious?
e) Was it told rather than memorized?

INTERVIEWING TECHNIQUES

a) Did the interviewer seem prepared?
b) Did the questions follow some sort of pattern?
c) Was the interviewer in charge?
d) Did the interview move along smoothly?
e) Did the interviewer get the interviewed to do most of the talking?
f) Was the vocabulary appropriate?

OUTLINE FOR EVALUATING PREPARED SPEECHES

a) Voice: loud, variety, flexible?
b) Use of language: interesting vocabulary?
c) Content: organization, beginning, middle, end?
d) General ability to interest listeners
(These could be marked on a scale of 1 to 10.)

ANOTHER OUTLINE FOR MARKING PREPARED SPEECHES

a) topic
b) audience contact
c) speech patterns (enunciation, pronunciation, etc.)
d) variety in voice
e) organization of material
f) originality of material
g) overall impression

All these suggestions lead to evaluating what has been taught at some time. In this way, we can find out how much the student has progressed. Equally, we can discover how well we have taught.

Reference: Books of Value When You Teach Whole Language

There are many, many excellent books about Reading, Writing, Listening, Speaking, Viewing and Doing.

Here are some books, published recently, which I have used:

Tell Me Another by Bob Barton. Dozens of ideas for story-telling, and many wonderful tales.

Choosing Children's Books by David Booth, Larry Swartz, Meguido Zola. This list of over 600 children's books will give you all kinds of ideas.

Games for Everyone by David Booth. Two hundred games for children of all ages.

Words That Taste Good by Bill Moore. Over 600 short pieces of poetry to use with your students.

Poems Please by David Booth and Bill Moore. How to share the pleasures of poetry. A classroom teacher's book.

Butterscotch Dreams by Sonja Dunn. More than 60 original chants, with hundreds of follow-up activities.

Playing With Words by Margie Golick. Over 50 word games for students of all ages.

Reading, Writing and Rummy by Margie Golick. Over a hundred card games, with specific learning skills for each game.

Dramathemes by Larry Swartz. Ten dramatic themes, and over a hundred specific drama lessons.

Media Scenes and Class Acts by Jack Livesley. How to explore all forms of media with students in the classroom.

Precision Reading by Ken Weber. Over 60 ways to help reluctant readers become proficient readers.

Canadian Scientists and Inventors by Bill Russell. A hundred Canadian inventors, with games and activities for the classroom.

Recognizing Richard Courtney. A series of ideas on drama in the classroom.

All these are published by Pembroke Publishers. They were all written by friends of mine. This makes the list very personal, subjective and biased. On the other hand, they are all excellent teachers, and their books are crammed with marvellous ideas.

Index